Heirloom Afghans
for Baby

By Terry Kimbrough

Table of Contents

General Instructions 1

1. Pristine 2

2. Timeless 3

3. Exquisite 7

4. Distinct 11

5. Enchanting 12

6. Charming 14

Leisure Arts Inc. • Maumelle Arkansas

GENERAL INSTRUCTIONS

ABBREVIATIONS

ch(s)   chain(s)
dc   double crochet(s)
hdc   half double crochet(s)
mm   millimeters
Rnd(s)   Round(s)
sc   single crochet(s)
sp(s)   space(s)
st(s)   stitch(es)
tr   treble crochet(s)
YO   yarn over

★ — work instructions following ★ as many **more** times as indicated in addition to the first time.

† to † — work all instructions from first † to second † **as many** times as specified.

( ) or **[ ]** — work enclosed instructions **as many** times as specified by the number immediately following **or** work all enclosed instructions in the stitch or space indicated **or** contains explanatory remarks.

colon (:) — the number(s) given after a colon at the end of a row or round denote(s) the number of stitches you should have on that row or round.

CROCHET TERMINOLOGY	
UNITED STATES	**INTERNATIONAL**
slip stitch (slip st) =	single crochet (sc)
single crochet (sc) =	double crochet (dc)
half double crochet (hdc) =	half treble crochet (htr)
double crochet (dc) =	treble crochet (tr)
treble crochet (tr) =	double treble crochet (dtr)
double treble crochet (dtr) =	triple treble crochet (ttr)
skip =	miss

ALUMINUM CROCHET HOOKS	
UNITED STATES	**METRIC (mm)**
B-1	2.25
C-2	2.75
D-3	3.25
E-4	3.50
F-5	3.75
G-6	4.00
H-8	5.00
I-9	5.50
J-10	6.00
K-10½	6.50
N	9.00
P	10.00
Q	15.00

GAUGE

Exact gauge is **essential** for proper size. Before beginning your project, make the sample swatch given in the individual instructions in the yarn and hook specified. After completing the swatch, measure it, counting your stitches and rows carefully. If your swatch is larger or smaller than specified, **make another, changing hook size to get the correct gauge**. Keep trying until you find the size hook that will give you the specified gauge.

BACK LOOP ONLY

Work only in loop(s) indicated by arrow *(Fig. 1)*.

Fig. 1

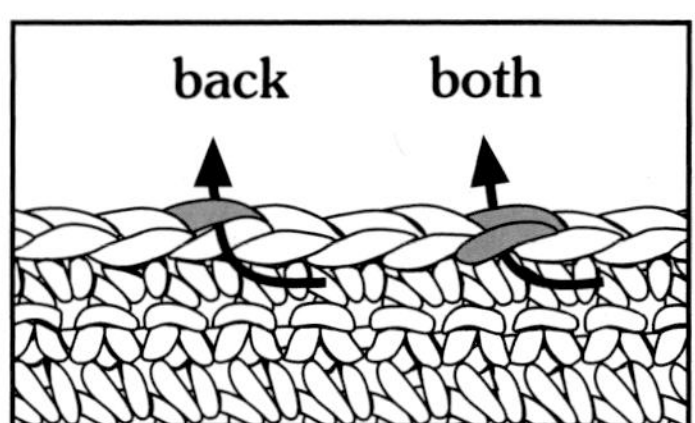

FREE LOOPS OF A CHAIN

When instructed to work in free loops of a chain, work in loop indicated by arrow *(Fig. 2)*.

Fig. 2

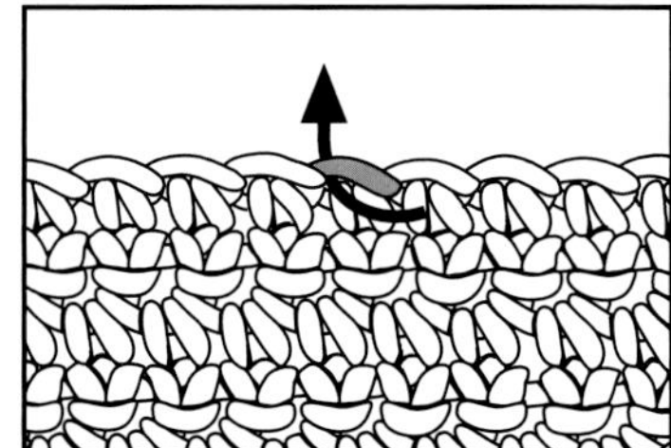

1. PRISTINE

Finished Size: 34¹/₂" x 46"

MATERIALS
Sport Weight Yarn:
20¹/₂ ounces, (580 grams, 1,640 yards)
Crochet hook, size H (5.00 mm) **or** size needed
for gauge

GAUGE: In pattern, one repeat (16 dc and 3 sps)
and 8¹/₂ rows = 5"

Gauge Swatch: 7"w x 5"h
Foundation Row: Ch 8, dc in fourth ch from hook to
form a ring, (ch 12, dc in fourth ch from hook to form a
ring) twice: 3 rings.
Row 1 (Right side): Ch 6, (4 dc, ch 2, 4 dc) around dc of
first ring, skip next 3 chs, dc in next ch, ch 1, dc in next
ch, work (dc, Picot, dc, ch 2, dc, Picot, dc) around dc of
next ring, skip next 3 chs, dc in next ch, ch 1, dc in next
ch, (4 dc, ch 2, 4 dc) around dc of next ring, skip next
3 chs, dc in last ch: 25 dc and 5 sps.
Row 2: Ch 6, turn; (sc, ch 3) twice in first ch-2 sp,
★ (dc, ch 1, dc) in next ch-1 sp, ch 3, (sc, ch 3) twice in
next ch-2 sp; repeat from ★ once **more**, skip last 4 dc,
dc in next ch: 11 sps.
Row 3: Ch 3, turn; skip first ch-3 sp, (4 dc, ch 2, 4 dc)
in next ch-3 sp, skip next ch-3 sp, (dc, ch 1, dc) in next
ch-1 sp, skip next ch-3 sp, work (dc, Picot, dc, ch 2, dc,
Picot, dc) in next ch-3 sp, skip next ch-3 sp, (dc, ch 1,
dc) in next ch-1 sp, skip next ch-3 sp, (4 dc, ch 2, 4 dc)
in next ch-3 sp, skip next 3 chs, dc in next ch: 25 dc and
5 sps.
Rows 4-8: Repeat Rows 2 and 3 twice, then repeat
Row 2 once **more**.
Finish off.

STITCH GUIDE

> **PICOT**
> Ch 3, sc in top of dc just made.

AFGHAN BODY
Foundation Row: Ch 8, dc in fourth ch from hook to
form a ring, (ch 12, dc in fourth ch from hook to form a
ring) 8 times: 9 rings.

Row 1 (Right side): Ch 6, place marker in third ch from
hook for st placement, (4 dc, ch 2, 4 dc) around dc of first
ring, skip next 3 chs, dc in next ch, ★ ch 1, dc in next ch,
work (dc, Picot, dc, ch 2, dc, Picot, dc) around dc of next
ring, skip next 3 chs, dc in next ch, ch 1, dc in next ch,
(4 dc, ch 2, 4 dc) around dc of next ring, skip next 3 chs,
dc in next ch; repeat from ★ across: 73 dc and 17 sps.

Row 2: Ch 6, turn; (sc, ch 3) twice in first ch-2 sp,
★ (dc, ch 1, dc) in next ch-1 sp, ch 3, (sc, ch 3) twice in
next ch-2 sp; repeat from ★ across to last 4 dc, skip last
4 dc, dc in next ch: 35 sps.

Row 3: Ch 3 (counts as first dc, now and
throughout), turn; skip first ch-3 sp, (4 dc, ch 2, 4 dc)
in next ch-3 sp, ★ skip next ch-3 sp, (dc, ch 1, dc) in next
ch-1 sp, skip next ch-3 sp, work (dc, Picot, dc, ch 2, dc,
Picot, dc) in next ch-3 sp, skip next ch-3 sp, (dc, ch 1,
dc) in next ch-1 sp, skip next ch-3 sp, (4 dc, ch 2, 4 dc)
in next ch-3 sp; repeat from ★ across to last sp, skip next
3 chs, dc in next ch: 74 dc and 17 sps.

Row 4: Ch 6, turn; (sc, ch 3) twice in first ch-2 sp,
★ (dc, ch 1, dc) in next ch-1 sp, ch 3, (sc, ch 3) twice in
next ch-2 sp; repeat from ★ across to last 5 dc, skip next
4 dc, dc in last dc: 35 sps.

Repeat Rows 3 and 4 until Afghan Body measures
approximately 32¹/₂" from beginning ch, ending by
working Row 3.

Last Row: Ch 6, turn; sc in first ch-2 sp, ch 3, ★ (dc,
ch 1, dc) in next ch-1 sp, ch 3, sc in next ch-2 sp, ch 3;
repeat from ★ across to last 5 dc, skip next 4 dc, dc in
last dc; do **not** finish off: 26 sps.

EDGING
Rnd 1: Ch 1, turn; sc in first dc, 4 sc in each of next
2 ch-3 sps, (sc in next ch-1 sp, 4 sc in each of next
2 ch-3 sps) across to last dc, sc in last dc, place marker
around sc just made for st placement; work 116 sc evenly
spaced across end of rows; working in free loops *(Fig. 2,
page 1)* and in sps across beginning ch, sc in first ch,
place marker around sc just made for st placement, 3 sc
in next sp, 2 sc in next sp, 3 sc in next sp, ★ sc in sp
between next 2 dc, 3 sc in next sp, 2 sc in next sp,
3 sc in next sp; repeat from ★ across to marked ch, sc in
marked ch, remove marker and place around sc just made
for st placement; work 116 sc evenly spaced across end
of rows; join with slip st to first sc: 396 sc.

Rnd 2: Ch 5 (counts as first dc plus ch 2, now and
throughout), do **not** turn; dc in same st and in next
3 sc, ch 2, ★ (skip next 2 sc, dc in next 4 sc, ch 2) across
to within 5 sc of marked sc, skip next 2 sc, dc in next
3 sc, (dc, ch 2, dc) in marked sc, remove marker, dc in
next 3 sc, ch 2; repeat from ★ 2 times **more**, (skip next
2 sc, dc in next 4 sc, ch 2) across to last 5 sc, skip next
2 sc, dc in last 3 sc; join with slip st to first dc: 272 dc
and 68 ch-2 sps.

Rnd 3: Ch 3, (3 dc, ch 2, 3 dc) in next corner ch-2 sp,
★ dc in next dc, ch 2, skip next 2 dc, dc in next dc, (2 dc
in next ch-2 sp, dc in next dc, ch 2, skip next 2 dc, dc in
next dc) across to next corner ch-2 sp, (3 dc, ch 2, 3 dc)
in corner ch-2 sp; repeat from ★ 2 times **more**, dc in
next dc, ch 2, skip next 2 dc, (dc in next dc, 2 dc in next
ch-2 sp, dc in next dc, ch 2, skip next 2 dc) across; join
with slip st to first dc: 288 dc and 72 ch-2 sps.

Rnd 4: Ch 5, skip next 2 dc, dc in next dc, (3 dc, ch 2,
3 dc) in next corner ch-2 sp, ★ dc in next dc, ch 2, skip
next 2 dc, dc in next dc, (2 dc in next ch-2 sp, dc in
next dc, ch 2, skip next 2 dc, dc in next dc) across to
next corner ch-2 sp, (3 dc, ch 2, 3 dc) in corner ch-2 sp;
repeat from ★ 2 times **more**, (dc in next dc, ch 2, skip
next 2 dc, dc in next dc, 2 dc in next ch-2 sp) across;
join with slip st to first dc, do **not** finish off: 304 dc and
76 ch-2 sps.

Continued on page 3."

Rnd 5: Slip st in first ch-2 sp, ch 5, 4 dc in same sp, (4 dc, ch 2, 4 dc) in next ch-2 sp and in each ch-2 sp around, 3 dc in same sp as first dc; join with slip st to first dc: 76 ch-2 sps.

Rnd 6: Slip st in first ch-2 sp, ch 5, 4 dc in same sp, skip next 4 dc, dc in sp **before** next dc, 4 dc in next corner ch-2 sp, (ch 2, 4 dc in same sp) twice, skip next 4 dc, dc in sp **before** next dc, ★ [(4 dc, ch 2, 4 dc) in next ch-2 sp, skip next 4 dc, dc in sp **before** next dc] across to next corner ch-2 sp, 4 dc in corner ch-2 sp, (ch 2, 4 dc in same sp) twice, skip next 4 dc, dc in sp **before** next dc; repeat from ★ 2 times **more**, [(4 dc, ch 2, 4 dc) in next ch-2 sp, skip next 4 dc, dc in sp **before** next dc] across, 3 dc in same sp as first dc; join with slip st to first dc: 80 ch-2 sps.

Rnd 7: Slip st in first ch-2 sp, ch 5, 4 dc in same sp, skip next 4 dc, dc in next dc, † (4 dc, ch 2, 4 dc) in next 2 ch-2 sps, skip next 4 dc, dc in next dc, [(4 dc, ch 2, 4 dc) in next ch-2 sp, skip next 4 dc, dc in next dc] 15 times, (4 dc, ch 2, 4 dc) in next 2 ch-2 sps, skip next 4 dc, dc in next dc †, [(4 dc, ch 2, 4 dc) in next ch-2 sp, skip next 4 dc, dc in next dc] 21 times, repeat from † to † once, [(4 dc, ch 2, 4 dc) in next ch-2 sp, skip next 4 dc, dc in next dc] across, 3 dc in same sp as first dc; join with slip st to first dc.

Rnd 8: Slip st in first ch-2 sp, ch 5, 4 dc in same sp, skip next 4 dc, dc in next dc, (4 dc, ch 2, 4 dc) in next ch-2 sp, skip next 4 dc, † (dc, ch 2, dc) in corner sp **before** next dc, (4 dc, ch 2, 4 dc) in next ch-2 sp, skip next 4 dc, [dc in next dc, (4 dc, ch 2, 4 dc) in next ch-2 sp, skip next 4 dc] 16 times, (dc, ch 2, dc) in corner sp **before** next dc †, (4 dc, ch 2, 4 dc) in next ch-2 sp, skip next 4 dc, [dc in next dc, (4 dc, ch 2, 4 dc) in next ch-2 sp, skip next 4 dc] 22 times, repeat from † to † once, [(4 dc, ch 2, 4 dc) in next ch-2 sp, skip next 4 dc, dc in next dc] across, 3 dc in same sp as first dc; join with slip st to first dc: 84 ch-2 sps.

Rnd 9: Slip st in first ch-2 sp, ch 5, 4 dc in same sp, [skip next 4 dc, dc in next dc, (4 dc, ch 2, 4 dc) in next ch-2 sp] twice, dc in next dc, ★ [(4 dc, ch 2, 4 dc) in next ch-2 sp, skip next 4 dc, dc in next dc] across to next corner ch-2 sp, (4 dc, ch 2, 4 dc) in corner ch-2 sp, dc in next dc; repeat from ★ 2 times **more**, [(4 dc, ch 2, 4 dc) in next ch-2 sp, skip next 4 dc, dc in next dc] across, 3 dc in same sp as first dc; join with slip st to first dc.

Rnd 10: Slip st in first ch-2 sp, ch 3, (3 dc, ch 2, 4 dc) in same sp, skip next 4 dc, dc in next dc, ★ (4 dc, ch 2, 4 dc) in next ch-2 sp, skip next 4 dc, dc in next dc; repeat from ★ around; join with slip st to first dc.

Rnd 11: Slip st in next dc, ch 1, sc in same st, ch 3, skip next dc, sc in next dc, ch 3, sc in next ch-2 sp, ch 3, sc in next dc, ch 3, skip next dc, sc in next dc, skip next 3 dc, ★ sc in next dc, ch 3, skip next dc, sc in next dc, ch 3, sc in next ch-2 sp, ch 3, sc in next dc, ch 3, skip next dc, sc in next dc, skip next 3 sts; repeat from ★ around; join with slip st to first sc, finish off.

2. TIMELESS

Finished Size: 34¹⁄₂" x 46"

MATERIALS
Sport Weight Yarn:
   17 ounces, (480 grams, 1,360 yards)
Crochet hook, size H (5.00 mm) **or** size needed
   for gauge

GAUGE: In pattern, 13 dc = 3"; 8 rows = 4"

Gauge Swatch: 4¹⁄₂"w x 4"h
Ch 23 **loosely**.
Work same as Afghan Body for 8 rows.
Finish off.

Note: Each row of Afghan Body is worked across length of Afghan.

STITCH GUIDE

TREBLE CROCHET *(abbreviated tr)*
YO twice, insert hook in sc indicated, YO and pull up a loop (4 loops on hook), (YO and draw through 2 loops on hook) 3 times.

2-DC CLUSTER (uses one ch-2 sp)
★ YO, insert hook in ch-2 sp indicated, YO and pull up a loop, YO and draw through 2 loops on hook; repeat from ★ once **more**, YO and draw through all 3 loops on hook.

3-DC CLUSTER (uses one sc)
★ YO, insert hook in sc indicated, YO and pull up a loop, YO and draw through 2 loops on hook; repeat from ★ 2 times **more**, YO and draw through all 4 loops on hook.

DECREASE
Pull up a loop in same sp **and** in next ch-5 sp, YO and draw through all 3 loops on hook.

PICOT
Ch 5, sc in third ch from hook, ch 2.

AFGHAN BODY
Ch 155 **loosely**, place marker in fifth ch from hook for st placement.

Row 1: Sc in eighth ch from hook, ch 2, skip next 2 chs, dc in next ch, ★ ch 2, skip next 2 chs, sc in next ch, ch 2, skip next 2 chs, dc in next ch; repeat from ★ across: 50 sts and 50 sps.

Row 2 (Right side)**:** Ch 1, turn; sc in first dc, ch 2, work 3-dc Cluster in next sc, ch 2, ★ sc in next dc, ch 2, work 3-dc Cluster in next sc, ch 2; repeat from ★ across to last sp, skip next 2 chs, sc in next ch: 51 sts and 50 ch-2 sps.

Row 3: Ch 5 **(counts as first dc plus ch 2, now and throughout)**, turn; sc in next 3-dc Cluster, ch 2, dc in next sc, ★ ch 2, sc in next 3-dc Cluster, ch 2, dc in next sc; repeat from ★ across.

Row 4: Ch 3 **(counts as first dc, now and throughout)**, turn; ★ 2 dc in next ch-2 sp, dc in next sc, 2 dc in next ch-2 sp, dc in next dc; repeat from ★ across: 151 dc.

Row 5: Ch 1, turn; sc in first dc, ★ ch 2, skip next 2 dc, (dc, ch 2) twice in next dc, skip next 2 dc, sc in next dc; repeat from ★ across: 76 sts and 75 ch-2 sps.

Row 6: Ch 4 **(counts as first tr)**, turn; skip next ch-2 sp, work 2-dc Cluster in next ch-2 sp, (ch 1, work 2-dc Cluster in same sp) twice, ★ ch 1, skip next 2 ch-2 sps, work 2-dc Cluster in next ch-2 sp, (ch 1, work 2-dc Cluster in same sp) twice; repeat from ★ across to last ch-2 sp, skip last ch-2 sp, tr in last sc: 77 sts and 74 ch-1 sps.

Row 7: Ch 4 **(counts as first dc plus ch 1)**, turn; (dc in next ch-1 sp, ch 1) across to last 2 sts, skip next 2-dc Cluster, dc in last tr: 76 dc and 75 ch-1 sps.

Row 8: Ch 3, turn; dc in each ch-1 sp and in each dc across: 151 dc.

Row 9: Ch 5, turn; skip next 2 dc, sc in next dc, ch 2, skip next 2 dc, dc in next dc, ★ ch 2, skip next 2 dc, sc in next dc, ch 2, skip next 2 dc, dc in next dc; repeat from ★ across: 51 sts and 50 ch-2 sps.

Repeat Rows 2-9 until Afghan Body measures approximately 24$\frac{1}{2}$" from beginning ch, ending by working Row 3; do **not** finish off.

EDGING

Rnd 1: Ch 1, turn; sc in first dc, 3 sc in next ch-2 sp, sc in next sc, ★ 2 sc in next ch-2 sp, sc in next dc, 2 sc in next ch-2 sp, sc in next sc; repeat from ★ across to last ch-2 sp, 3 sc in last ch-2 sp, sc in last dc, place marker around sc just made for st placement; work 103 sc evenly spaced across end of rows; working in free loops *(Fig. 2, page 1)* and in sps across beginning ch, sc in marked ch, remove marker and place around sc just made for st placement, 3 sc in next sp, sc in next ch, (2 sc in next sp, sc in next ch) across to last sp, 3 sc in last sp, sc in last ch, place marker around sc just made for st placement; work 103 sc evenly spaced across end of rows; join with slip st to first sc: 512 sc.

Rnd 2: Ch 4 **(counts as first dc plus ch 1, now and throughout)**, do **not** turn; dc in same st, ch 1, ★ skip next sc, (dc in next sc, ch 1, skip next sc) across to next marked sc, (dc, ch 1) 3 times in marked sc, remove marker; repeat from ★ 2 times **more**, skip next sc, (dc in next sc, ch 1, skip next sc) across, dc in same st as first dc, ch 1; join with slip st to first dc: 264 dc.

Rnd 3: Ch 4, dc in same st, ch 1, ★ (dc in next dc, ch 1) across to next corner dc, (dc, ch 1) 3 times in corner dc; repeat from ★ 2 times **more**, (dc in next dc, ch 1) across, dc in same st as first dc, ch 1; join with slip st to first dc: 272 dc and 272 ch-1 sps.

Rnd 4: Ch 1, 2 sc in same st and in next ch-1 sp, ★ sc in next dc and in each ch-1 sp and each dc across to within one ch-1 sp of next corner dc, 2 sc in next ch-1 sp, 3 sc in corner dc, 2 sc in next ch-1 sp; repeat from ★ 2 times **more**, sc in next dc and in each ch-1 sp and each dc across to last ch-1 sp, 2 sc in last ch-1 sp, sc in same st as first sc; join with slip st to first sc: 560 sc.

Rnd 5: Ch 5, dc in same st, (dc, ch 2, dc) in next sc, ★ [ch 2, skip next 2 sc, sc in next sc, ch 2, skip next 2 sc, (dc, ch 2, dc) in next sc] across to center sc of next corner 3-sc group, (dc, ch 2, dc) in center sc and in next sc; repeat from ★ 2 times **more**, [ch 2, skip next 2 sc, sc in next sc, ch 2, skip next 2 sc, (dc, ch 2, dc) in next sc] across; join with slip st to first dc: 284 ch-2 sps.

Rnd 6: (Slip st, ch 2, dc) in first ch-2 sp, ch 1, (work 2-dc Cluster in same sp, ch 1) twice, (work 2-dc Cluster, ch 1) 3 times in next ch-2 sp, ★ [skip next 2 ch-2 sps, (work 2-dc Cluster, ch 1) 3 times in next ch-2 sp] across to next corner ch-2 sp, (work 2-dc Cluster, ch 1) 3 times in corner ch-2 sp and in next ch-2 sp; repeat from ★ 2 times **more**, [skip next 2 ch-2 sps, (work 2-dc Cluster, ch 1) 3 times in next ch-2 sp] across; join with slip st to first dc: 300 ch-1 sps.

Rnd 7: Slip st in first ch-1 sp, ch 5, dc in same sp, (dc, ch 2) twice in next ch-1 sp, † [skip next ch-1 sp, (dc, ch 2, dc) in next 2 ch-1 sps] 28 times, ch 2, skip next ch-1 sp, (dc, ch 2, dc) in next 2 ch-1 sps, ch 2, [skip next ch-1 sp, (dc, ch 2, dc) in next 2 ch-1 sps] 20 times, ch 2, skip next ch-1 sp †, (dc, ch 2, dc) in next 2 ch-1 sps, ch 2, repeat from † to † once; join with slip st to first dc: 208 ch-2 sps.

Rnd 8: Slip st in first ch-2 sp, ch 1, sc in same sp, (ch 5, sc in next ch-2 sp) around, ch 2, dc in first sc to form last ch-5 sp.

Rnd 9: Ch 1, sc in same sp, (ch 5, sc in next ch-5 sp) around, ch 4, sc in first sc to form last ch-5 sp.

Rnd 10: (Decrease, work Picot) around; join with slip st to first decrease, finish off.

5
5

6
6

3. EXQUISITE

Finished Size: 37" x 46"

MATERIALS
Sport Weight Yarn:
  $17^1/_2$ ounces, (500 grams, 1,400 yards)
Crochet hook, size H (5.00 mm) **or** size needed
  for gauge

GAUGE: In pattern, one repeat = $3^1/_4$";
  8 rows = $3^3/_4$"

Gauge Swatch: $6^1/_2$"w x $2^1/_2$"h
Ch 28 **loosely**.
Work same as Afghan Body for 5 rows.
Finish off.

STITCH GUIDE

> **TREBLE CROCHET** (*abbreviated tr*)
> YO twice, insert hook in st or sp indicated, YO and
> pull up a loop (4 loops on hook), (YO and draw
> through 2 loops on hook) 3 times.
>
> **PICOT**
> Ch 3, sc in top of last dc made.
>
> **CLUSTER** (uses one st or sp)
> ★ YO, insert hook in st or sp indicated, YO and pull
> up a loop, YO and draw through 2 loops on hook;
> repeat from ★ once **more**, YO and draw through all
> 3 loops on hook.

AFGHAN BODY
Ch 93 **loosely**.

Row 1: Sc in second ch from hook and in next ch, ch 3,
skip next 2 chs, sc in next ch, ch 5, skip next 4 chs, sc in
next ch, ch 3, ★ skip next 2 chs, sc in next 3 chs, ch 3,
skip next 2 chs, sc in next ch, ch 5, skip next 4 chs, sc
in next ch, ch 3; repeat from ★ across to last 4 chs, skip
next 2 chs, sc in last 2 chs: 21 sps.

Row 2 (Right side)**:** Ch 1, turn; sc in first sc, ch 1, ★ sc
in next ch-3 sp, ch 2, 7 dc in next ch-5 sp, ch 2, sc in
next ch-3 sp, ch 1; repeat from ★ across to last 2 sc, skip
next sc, sc in last sc: 65 sts and 22 sps.

Row 3: Ch 3 **(counts as first dc, now and
throughout)**, turn; dc in next ch-1 sp, skip next sc,
dc in next dc, (ch 1, dc in next dc) 6 times, ★ skip next
ch-2 sp, (dc, work Picot, dc) in next sp, skip next sc, dc
in next dc, (ch 1, dc in next dc) 6 times; repeat from ★
across to last 2 sps, skip next ch-2 sp, dc in next ch-1 sp
and in last sc: 42 ch-1 sps.

Row 4: Ch 1, turn; sc in first dc, ch 1, sc in next
ch-1 sp, (ch 3, sc in next ch-1 sp) 5 times, ★ ch 5, skip
next Picot, sc in next ch-1 sp, (ch 3, sc in next ch-1 sp) 5
times; repeat from ★ across to last 3 dc, ch 1, skip next
2 dc, sc in last dc: 43 sps.

Row 5: Ch 3, turn; dc in next ch-1 sp, ch 3, skip next
ch-3 sp, sc in next ch-3 sp, ch 5, skip next ch-3 sp, sc in
next ch-3 sp, ch 3, ★ skip next ch-3 sp, (dc, work Picot,
dc) in next ch-5 sp, ch 3, skip next ch-3 sp, sc in next
ch-3 sp, ch 5, skip next ch-3 sp, sc in next ch-3 sp, ch 3;
repeat from ★ across to last 2 sps, skip next ch-3 sp, dc
in next ch-1 sp and in last sc: 21 sps.

Row 6: Ch 1, turn; sc in first dc, ch 1, sc in next
ch-3 sp, ch 2, 7 dc in next ch-5 sp, ch 2, sc in next
ch-3 sp, ★ ch 5, skip next Picot, sc in next ch-3 sp, ch 2,
7 dc in next ch-5 sp, ch 2, sc in next ch-3 sp; repeat
from ★ across to last 2 dc, ch 1, skip next dc, sc in last
dc: 65 sts and 22 sps.

Repeat Rows 3-6 until Afghan Body measures
approximately $30^1/_2$" from beginning ch, ending by
working Row 4.

Last Row: Ch 3, turn; dc in next ch-1 sp, ch 2, skip
next ch-3 sp, sc in next ch-3 sp, ch 4, skip next ch-3 sp,
sc in next ch-3 sp, ch 2, ★ skip next ch-3 sp, (dc, ch 1,
dc) in next ch-5 sp, ch 2, skip next ch-3 sp, sc in next
ch-3 sp, ch 4, skip next ch-3 sp, sc in next ch-3 sp, ch 2;
repeat from ★ across to last 2 sps, skip next ch-3 sp, dc
in next ch-1 sp and in last sc; do **not** finish off.

EDGING
Rnd 1: Ch 1, turn; work 85 sc evenly spaced across
to next corner, place marker around last sc made for st
placement; work 115 sc evenly spaced across end of
rows; working in free loops *(Fig. 2, page 1)* and in sps
across beginning ch, sc in ch at base of first sc, place
marker around sc just made for st placement, work
84 sc evenly spaced across to next corner, place marker
around last sc made for st placement; work 115 sc
evenly spaced across end of rows; join with slip st to first
sc: 400 sc.

Rnd 2: Ch 2, do **not** turn; (dc, ch 2, work Cluster) in
same st, ch 1, skip next sc, (tr, ch 3, tr) in next sc, ch 1,
★ [skip next 3 sc, (dc, work Picot, dc) in next sc, ch 1,
skip next 3 sc, work (Cluster, ch 2, Cluster) in next sc,
ch 1, skip next 3 sc, (dc, work Picot, dc) in next sc,
ch 1, skip next 3 sc, (tr, ch 3, tr) in next sc, ch 1] across
to within one sc of next marked sc, skip next sc, work
(Cluster, ch 2, Cluster) in marked sc, ch 1, skip next
sc, (tr, ch 3, tr) in next sc, ch 1; repeat from ★ 2 times
more, [skip next 3 sc, (dc, work Picot, dc) in next sc,
ch 1, skip next 3 sc, work (Cluster, ch 2, Cluster) in next
sc, ch 1, skip next 3 sc, (dc, work Picot, dc) in next sc,
ch 1, skip next 3 sc, (tr, ch 3, tr) in next sc, ch 1] across
to last sc, skip last sc; join with slip st to first dc: 160 sps.

Rnd 3: Slip st in first corner ch-2 sp, ch 2, (dc, ch 2,
work Cluster) in same sp, ch 2, ★ † skip next ch-1 sp,
9 tr in next ch-3 sp, ch 2, [skip next 2 ch-1 sps, (work
Cluster, ch 2) twice in next ch-2 sp, skip next 2 ch-1 sps,
9 tr in next ch-3 sp, ch 2] across to within one ch-1 sp of
next corner ch-2 sp, skip next ch-1 sp †, (work Cluster,
ch 2) twice in corner ch-2 sp; repeat from ★ 2 times
more, then repeat from † to † once; join with slip st to
first dc: 28 9-tr groups and 84 ch-2 sps.

Rnd 4: Slip st in first corner ch-2 sp, ch 2, (dc, ch 2, work Cluster) in same sp, ch 2, ★ † skip next Cluster, dc in next tr, (ch 1, dc in next tr) 8 times, ch 2, [skip next ch-2 sp, (work Cluster, ch 2) twice in next ch-2 sp, skip next Cluster, dc in next tr, (ch 1, dc in next tr) 8 times, ch 2] across to within one ch-2 sp of next corner ch-2 sp, skip next ch-2 sp †, (work Cluster, ch 2) 3 times in corner ch-2 sp; repeat from ★ 2 times **more**, then repeat from † to † once, work Cluster in same sp as first slip st, ch 2; join with slip st to first dc: 312 sps.

Rnd 5: Slip st in first ch-2 sp, ch 2, (dc, ch 2, work Cluster) in same sp, ch 2, ★ † skip next ch-2 sp, sc in next ch-1 sp, (ch 3, sc in next ch-1 sp) 7 times, ch 2, [skip next ch-2 sp, (work Cluster, ch 2) twice in next ch-2 sp, skip next ch-2 sp, sc in next ch-1 sp, (ch 3, sc in next ch-1 sp) 7 times, ch 2] across within 2 ch-2 sps of next corner Cluster, skip next ch-2 sp, work (Cluster, ch 2, Cluster) in next ch-2 sp, ch 3 †, (work Cluster, ch 2) twice in next ch-2 sp; repeat from ★ 2 times **more**, then repeat from † to † once; join with slip st to first dc: 288 sps.

Rnd 6: Slip st in first ch-2 sp, ch 2, (dc, ch 2, work Cluster) in same sp, ch 2, ★ † skip next ch-2 sp, sc in next ch-3 sp, (ch 3, sc in next ch-3 sp) 6 times, ch 2, [skip next ch-2 sp, (work Cluster, ch 2) twice in next ch-2 sp, skip next ch-2 sp, sc in next ch-3 sp, (ch 3, sc in next ch-3 sp) 6 times, ch 2] across within 2 ch-2 sps of next corner ch-3 sp, skip next ch-2 sp, work (Cluster, ch 2, Cluster) in next ch-2 sp, ch 3, (sc, ch 3) twice in corner ch-3 sp †, (work Cluster, ch 2) twice in next ch-2 sp; repeat from ★ 2 times **more**, then repeat from † to † once; join with slip st to first dc: 268 sps.

Rnd 7: Slip st in first ch-2 sp, ch 2, (dc, ch 2, work Cluster) in same sp, ch 2, ★ † skip next ch-2 sp, sc in next ch-3 sp, (ch 3, sc in next ch-3 sp) 5 times, ch 2, [skip next ch-2 sp, (work Cluster, ch 2) 3 times in next ch-2 sp, skip next ch-2 sp, sc in next ch-3 sp, (ch 3, sc in next ch-3 sp) 5 times, ch 2] across within 3 sps of next corner ch-3 sp, skip next ch-2 sp, [work (Cluster, ch 2, Cluster) in next sp, ch 3, sc in next ch-3 sp, ch 3] twice †, (work Cluster, ch 2) twice in next ch-2 sp; repeat from ★ 2 times **more**, then repeat from † to † once; join with slip st to first dc: 272 sps.

Rnd 8: Slip st in first ch-2 sp, ch 2, (dc, ch 2, work Cluster) in same sp, ch 2, ★ † skip next ch-2 sp, sc in next ch-3 sp, (ch 3, sc in next ch-3 sp) 4 times, ch 2, [skip next ch-2 sp, work (Cluster, ch 2, Cluster) in next ch-2 sp, ch 3, (work Cluster, ch 2) twice in next ch-2 sp, skip next ch-2 sp, sc in next ch-3 sp, (ch 3, sc in next ch-3 sp) 4 times, ch 2] across within 4 sps of next corner ch-2 sp, skip next ch-2 sp, [work (Cluster, ch 2, Cluster) in next ch-2 sp, ch 3, (sc in next ch-3 sp, ch 3) twice] 2 times †, (work Cluster, ch 2) twice in next ch-2 sp; repeat from ★ 2 times **more**, then repeat from † to † once; join with slip st to first dc: 276 sps.

Rnd 9: Slip st in first ch-2 sp, ch 2, (dc, ch 2, work Cluster) in same sp, ch 2, ★ † skip next ch-2 sp, sc in next ch-3 sp, (ch 3, sc in next ch-3 sp) 3 times, ch 2, [skip next ch-2 sp, (work Cluster, ch 2) twice in next ch-2 sp, (dc, ch 3, dc) in next ch-3 sp, ch 2, (work Cluster, ch 2) twice in next ch-2 sp, skip next ch-2 sp, sc in next ch-3 sp, (ch 3, sc in next ch-3 sp) 3 times, ch 2] across within 5 sps of next corner ch-2 sp, skip next ch-2 sp, [(work Cluster, ch 2) twice in next ch-2 sp, skip next ch-3 sp, (dc, ch 3, dc) in next ch-3 sp, ch 2, skip next ch-3 sp] twice †, (work Cluster, ch 2) twice in next ch-2 sp; repeat from ★ 2 times **more**, then repeat from † to † once; join with slip st to first dc: 296 sps.

Rnd 10: Slip st in first ch-2 sp, ch 2, (dc, ch 2, work Cluster) in same sp, ch 2, ★ † skip next ch-2 sp, sc in next ch-3 sp, (ch 3, sc in next ch-3 sp) twice, ch 2, [skip next ch-2 sp, (work Cluster, ch 2) twice in next ch-2 sp, skip next ch-2 sp, 7 dc in next ch-3 sp, ch 2, skip next ch-2 sp, (work Cluster, ch 2) twice in next ch-2 sp, skip next ch-2 sp, sc in next ch-3 sp, (ch 3, sc in next ch-3 sp) twice, ch 2] across within 5 sps of next corner ch-2 sp, skip next ch-2 sp, [(work Cluster, ch 2) twice in next ch-2 sp, skip next ch-2 sp, 7 dc in next ch-3 sp, ch 2, skip next ch-2 sp] twice †, (work Cluster, ch 2) twice in next ch-2 sp; repeat from ★ 2 times **more**, then repeat from † to † once; join with slip st to first dc: 32 7-dc groups and 236 sps.

Rnd 11: Slip st in first ch-2 sp, ch 2, (dc, ch 2, work Cluster) in same sp, ch 2, ★ † skip next ch-2 sp, sc in next ch-3 sp, ch 3, sc in next ch-3 sp, ch 2, [skip next ch-2 sp, (work Cluster, ch 2) twice in next ch-2 sp, skip next Cluster, dc in next dc, (ch 1, dc in next dc) 6 times, ch 2, skip next ch-2 sp, (work Cluster, ch 2) twice in next ch-2 sp, skip next ch-2 sp, sc in next ch-3 sp, ch 3, sc in next ch-3 sp, ch 2] across within 4 ch-2 sps of next corner ch-2 sp, skip next ch-2 sp, [(work Cluster, ch 2) twice in next ch-2 sp, skip next Cluster, dc in next dc, (ch 1, dc in next dc) 6 times, ch 2, skip next ch-2 sp] twice †, (work Cluster, ch 2) twice in next ch-2 sp; repeat from ★ 2 times **more**, then repeat from † to † once; join with slip st to first dc: 400 sps.

Rnd 12: Slip st in first ch-2 sp, ch 2, dc in same sp, ★ † skip next 3 sps, work Cluster in next ch-2 sp, ch 3, sc in third ch from hook, skip next Cluster, (dc in next dc, ch 3, sc in third ch from hook) 7 times, [skip next ch-2 sp, work Cluster in next ch-2 sp, skip next 3 sps, work Cluster in next ch-2 sp, ch 3, sc in third ch from hook, skip next Cluster, (dc in next dc, ch 3, sc in third ch from hook) 7 times] across to within one ch-2 sp of next corner ch-2 sp, skip next ch-2 sp, (work Cluster, ch 3, sc in third ch from hook) twice in corner ch-2 sp, skip next Cluster, (dc in next dc, ch 3, sc in third ch from hook) 7 times, skip next ch-2 sp †, work Cluster in next ch-2 sp; repeat from ★ 2 times **more**, then repeat from † to † once; join with slip st to first dc, finish off.

4

4. DISTINCT

Finished Size: 34$\frac{1}{2}$" x 45$\frac{1}{2}$"

MATERIALS
Sport Weight Yarn:
   19 ounces, (540 grams, 1,520 yards)
   Crochet hook, size H (5.00 mm) **or** size needed
      for gauge

GAUGE: In pattern, (dc, ch 1, dc) 5 times = 3$\frac{1}{2}$";
            7 rows = 4"

Gauge Swatch: 5$\frac{1}{2}$"w x 3$\frac{1}{2}$"h
Ch 26 **loosely**.
Work same as Afghan Body for 6 rows.
Finish off.

STITCH GUIDE

TREBLE CROCHET *(abbreviated tr)*
YO twice, insert hook in ch-1 sp indicated, YO and
pull up a loop (4 loops on hook), (YO and draw
through 2 loops on hook) 3 times.

PUFF STITCH *(abbreviated Puff St)*
★ YO, insert hook in st or sp indicated, YO and pull
up a $\frac{3}{4}$" loop; repeat from ★ 3 times **more** (9 loops
on hook), YO and draw through 8 loops on hook,
YO and draw through both loops on hook.

PICOT
Ch 3, sc in third ch from hook.

AFGHAN BODY
Ch 110 **loosely**, place marker in third ch from hook for
st placement.

Row 1 (Right side)**:** Dc in fifth ch from hook, ★ ch 1,
dc in next ch, skip next ch, dc in next ch; repeat from ★
across: 71 sts and 36 sps.

Row 2: Ch 3 **(counts as first dc, now and
throughout)**, turn; (dc, ch 1, dc) in next ch-1 sp, ch 2,
dc in next ch-1 sp, ch 2, ★ tr in next ch-1 sp, ch 2, dc in
next ch-1 sp, ch 2; repeat from ★ across to last ch-1 sp,
(dc, ch 1, dc) in last ch-1 sp, skip next dc, dc in next ch:
39 sts and 36 sps.

Row 3: Ch 3, turn; (dc, ch 1, dc) in next ch-1 sp, ch 2,
skip next dc, work Puff St in next dc, ★ ch 3, sc in next
tr, ch 3, work Puff St in next dc; repeat from ★ across to
last 2 sps, ch 2, skip next ch-2 sp, (dc, ch 1, dc) in last
ch-1 sp, skip next dc, dc in last dc.

Row 4: Ch 3, turn; (dc, ch 1, dc) in next ch-1 sp, ch 2,
skip next ch-2 sp, (dc in next ch-3 sp, ch 2) across to last
2 sps, skip next ch-2 sp, (dc, ch 1, dc) in last ch-1 sp,
skip next dc, dc in last dc: 38 dc and 35 sps.

Rows 5-7: Ch 3, turn; (dc, ch 1, dc) in each sp across
to last 2 dc, skip next dc, dc in last dc: 72 dc and
35 ch-1 sps.

Row 8: Ch 3, turn; (dc, ch 1, dc) in next ch-1 sp, ch 2,
dc in next ch-1 sp, ch 2, ★ tr in next ch-1 sp, ch 2, dc in
next ch-1 sp, ch 2; repeat from ★ across to last ch-1 sp,
(dc, ch 1, dc) in last ch-1 sp, skip next dc, dc in last dc:
39 sts and 36 sps.

Repeat Rows 3-8 until Afghan Body measures
approximately 36" from beginning ch, ending by working
Row 5; do **not** finish off.

EDGING
Rnd 1: Ch 1, do **not** turn; sc in top of last dc on last
row, work 122 sc evenly spaced across end of rows;
working in free loops *(Fig. 2, page 1)* and in sps across
beginning ch, sc in first ch, place marker around sc just
made for st placement, work 86 sc evenly spaced across
to marked ch, sc in marked ch, remove marker and
place around sc just made for st placement; work 122 sc
evenly spaced across end of rows; working across last
row, sc in first dc, place marker around sc just made for
st placement, work 86 sc evenly spaced across; join with
slip st to first sc: 420 sc.

Rnd 2: Ch 1, (sc, ch 5) twice in same st, ★ skip next
2 sc, (sc in next sc, ch 5, skip next 2 sc) across to next
marked sc, (sc, ch 5) twice in marked sc, remove marker;
repeat from ★ 2 times **more**, skip next 2 sc, sc in next
sc, (ch 5, skip next 2 sc, sc in next sc) across to last 2 sc,
ch 2, skip last 2 sc, dc in first sc to form last ch-5 sp:
144 ch-5 sps.

Rnd 3: Ch 1, sc in same sp, work Puff St in next corner
ch-5 sp, (ch 5, work Puff St in same sp) 4 times, sc in
next ch-5 sp, ch 3, ★ † sc in next ch-5 sp, work Puff St
in next ch-5 sp, (ch 5, work Puff St in same sp) twice,
sc in next ch-5 sp, ch 3 †, repeat from † to † across to
within one ch-5 sp of next corner ch-5 sp, sc in next
ch-5 sp, work Puff St in corner ch-5 sp, (ch 5, work
Puff St in same sp) 4 times, sc in next ch-5 sp, ch 3;
repeat from ★ 2 times **more**, then repeat from † to †
across; join with slip st to first sc: 152 sps.

Rnd 4: Slip st in first Puff St and in next 2 chs, ch 1, (sc, ch 5) twice in same ch-5 sp and in next 2 ch-5 sps, † (sc, ch 5, sc) in next ch-5 sp, sc in next ch-3 sp, [(sc, ch 5) twice in next ch-5 sp, (sc, ch 5, sc) in next ch-5 sp, sc in next ch-3 sp] 13 times, (sc, ch 5) twice in next 2 ch-5 sps, place marker around last ch-5 made for st placement, [(sc, ch 5) twice in next ch-5 sp, (sc, ch 5, sc) in next ch-5 sp, sc in next ch-3 sp] 10 times †, (sc, ch 5) twice in next 2 ch-5 sps, place marker around last ch-5 made for st placement, (sc, ch 5) twice in next ch-5 sp, repeat from † to † once; join with slip st to first sc: 160 ch-5 sps.

Rnd 5: Slip st in next 2 chs, ch 1, sc in same ch-5 sp, work Puff St in next ch-5 sp, (ch 5, work Puff St in same sp) twice, (sc in next ch-5 sp, ch 3) twice, ★ † sc in next ch-5 sp, work Puff St in next ch-5 sp, (ch 5, work Puff St in same sp) twice, sc in next ch-5 sp, ch 3 †, repeat from † to † across to next marked ch-5 sp, sc in marked ch-5 sp, remove marker and place around last ch-3 made for st placement, ch 3; repeat from ★ 2 times **more**, then repeat from † to † across; join with slip st to first sc.

Rnd 6: Slip st in first Puff St and in next 2 chs, ch 1, (sc, ch 5) twice in same ch-5 sp and in next ch-5 sp, (sc in next ch-3 sp, ch 5) twice, (sc, ch 5) twice in next ch-5 sp, (sc, ch 5, sc) in next ch-5 sp, ★ [sc in next ch-3 sp, (sc, ch 5) twice in next ch-5 sp, (sc, ch 5, sc) in next ch-5 sp] across to next marked ch-3 sp, (ch 5, sc in next ch-3 sp) twice, (ch 5, sc) twice in next 2 ch-5 sps; repeat from ★ 2 times **more**, sc in next ch-3 sp, [(sc, ch 5) twice in next ch-5 sp, (sc, ch 5, sc) in next ch-5 sp, sc in next ch-3 sp] across; join with slip st to first sc, remove all markers: 168 ch-5 sps.

Rnd 7: Slip st in next 2 chs, ch 1, sc in same ch-5 sp, work Puff St in next ch-5 sp, (ch 5, work Puff St in same sp) twice, sc in next ch-5 sp, ch 3, ★ sc in next ch-5 sp, work Puff St in next ch-5 sp, (ch 5, work Puff St in same sp) twice, sc in next ch-5 sp, ch 3; repeat from ★ around; join with slip st to first sc.

Rnd 8: Slip st in first Puff St and in next ch-5 sp, ch 1, (sc in same sp, work Picot) 3 times, sc in next ch-5 sp, (work Picot, sc in same sp) twice, sc in next ch-3 sp, ★ (sc, work Picot) 3 times in next ch-5 sp, sc in next ch-5 sp, (work Picot, sc in same sp) twice, sc in next ch-3 sp; repeat from ★ around; join with slip st to first sc, finish off.

5. ENCHANTING

Finished Size: 33^1/$_2$" x 45^1/$_2$"

MATERIALS
Sport Weight Yarn:
16 ounces, (450 grams, 1,280 yards)
Crochet hook, size H (5.00 mm) **or** size needed
for gauge

GAUGE: In pattern, two repeats = 4^1/$_4$";
7 rows = 3^1/$_2$"

Gauge Swatch: 4^3/$_4$"w x 2^3/$_4$"h
Ch 26 **loosely**.
Work same as Afghan Body for 5 rows.
Finish off.

STITCH GUIDE

BEGINNING CLUSTER (uses one dc)
Ch 2, ★ YO, insert hook in dc indicated, YO and pull up a loop, YO and draw through 2 loops on hook; repeat from ★ once **more**, YO and draw through all 3 loops on hook.

CLUSTER (uses one st or sp)
★ YO, insert hook in st or sp indicated, YO and pull up a loop, YO and draw through 2 loops on hook; repeat from ★ 2 times **more**, YO and draw through all 4 loops on hook.

DECREASE
Pull up a loop in next 2 ch-1 sps, YO and draw through all 3 loops on hook.

AFGHAN BODY
Ch 96 **loosely**, place marker in fourth ch from hook for st placement.

Row 1: Dc in sixth ch from hook, ★ ch 1, skip next ch, dc in next ch; repeat from ★ across: 46 dc and 46 sps.

Row 2 (Right side)**:** Ch 4 **(counts as first dc plus ch 1, now and throughout)**, turn; ★ dc in next dc, ch 3, skip next dc, work Cluster in next dc, ch 3, skip next dc, dc in next dc, ch 1; repeat from ★ across to last sp, skip next ch, dc in next ch; do **not** finish off: 29 sts and 28 sps.

Continued on page 13.

Row 3: Ch 4, turn; dc in next dc, ★ ch 2, (sc in next ch-3 sp, ch 2) twice, dc in next dc, ch 1, dc in next dc; repeat from ★ across: 38 sts and 37 sps.

Row 4: Ch 4, turn; dc in next dc, ★ ch 3, skip next ch-2 sp, work Cluster in next ch-2 sp, ch 3, skip next sc, dc in next dc, ch 1, dc in next dc; repeat from ★ across: 29 sts and 28 sps.

Row 5: Ch 4, turn; dc in next dc, ★ ch 1, dc in next ch-3 sp, ch 1, dc in next Cluster, ch 1, dc in next ch-3 sp, (ch 1, dc in next dc) twice; repeat from ★ across: 47 dc and 46 ch-1 sps.

Row 6: Ch 4, turn; dc in next dc, ★ ch 3, skip next dc, work Cluster in next dc, ch 3, skip next dc, dc in next dc, ch 1, dc in next dc; repeat from ★ across: 29 sts and 28 sps.

Repeat Rows 3-6 until Afghan Body measures approximately 33" from beginning ch, ending by working Row 5; do **not** finish off.

EDGING

Rnd 1: Ch 1, turn; sc in first dc and in each ch-1 sp and each dc across to next corner, place marker around last sc made for st placement; work 127 sc evenly spaced across end of rows; working in free loops *(Fig. 2, page 1)* and in sps across beginning ch, sc in marked ch, remove marker and place around sc just made for st placement, sc in each sp and in ch at base of each dc across, place marker around last sc made for st placement; work 127 sc evenly spaced across end of rows; join with slip st to first sc: 440 sc.

Rnd 2: Ch 3 **(counts as first dc, now and throughout)**, do **not** turn; 2 dc in same st, ★ dc in each sc across to next marked sc, 5 dc in marked sc, remove marker; repeat from ★ 2 times **more**, dc in each sc across, 2 dc in same st as first dc; join with slip st to first dc: 456 dc.

Rnd 3: Work (Beginning Cluster, ch 2, Cluster) in same st, ch 2, ★ skip next 2 dc, (work Cluster in next dc, ch 2, skip next 2 dc) across to center dc of next corner 5-dc group, work (Cluster, ch 2) 3 times in center dc; repeat from ★ 2 times **more**, skip next 2 dc, (work Cluster in next dc, ch 2, skip next 2 dc) across, work Cluster in same st as Beginning Cluster, ch 2; join with slip st to top of Beginning Cluster: 160 Clusters.

Rnd 4: Ch 5 **(counts as first dc plus ch 2, now and throughout)**, dc in same st, ch 2, ★ (dc in next Cluster, ch 2) across to next corner Cluster, (dc, ch 2) 3 times in corner Cluster; repeat from ★ 2 times **more**, (dc in next Cluster, ch 2) across, dc in same st as first dc, ch 2; join with slip st to first dc: 168 dc.

Rnd 5: Ch 5, dc in same st, ch 2, ★ (dc in next dc, ch 2) across to next corner dc, (dc, ch 2) 3 times in corner dc; repeat from ★ 2 times **more**, (dc in next dc, ch 2) across, dc in same st as first dc, ch 2; join with slip st to first dc: 176 dc and 176 ch-2 sps.

Rnd 6: Ch 1, 2 sc in same st and in next ch-2 sp, ★ (sc in next dc, 2 sc in next ch-2 sp) across to next corner dc, 3 sc in corner dc, 2 sc in next ch-2 sp; repeat from ★ 2 times **more**, (sc in next dc, 2 sc in next ch-2 sp) across, sc in same st as first sc; join with slip st to first sc: 536 sc.

Rnd 7: Ch 3, 2 dc in same st, (dc in each sc across to center sc of next corner 3-sc group, 5 dc in center sc) 3 times, dc in each sc across, 2 dc in same st as first dc; join with slip st to first dc: 552 dc.

Rnd 8: Ch 4, dc in same st, ch 1, ★ skip next dc, (dc in next dc, ch 1, skip next dc) across to center dc of next corner 5-dc group, (dc, ch 1) 3 times in center dc; repeat from ★ 2 times **more**, skip next dc, (dc in next dc, ch 1, skip next dc) across, dc in same st as first dc, ch 1; join with slip st to first dc: 284 dc and 284 ch-1 sps.

Rnds 9 and 10: Ch 4, dc in same st, ch 1, ★ (dc in next dc, ch 1) across to next corner dc, (dc, ch 1) 3 times in corner dc; repeat from ★ 2 times **more**, (dc in next dc, ch 1) across, dc in same st as first dc, ch 1; join with slip st to first dc: 300 dc.

Rnd 11: Work [Beginning Cluster, (ch 3, Cluster) twice] in same st, ch 1, skip next dc, sc in next dc, ch 3, skip next dc, sc in next dc, ch 1, skip next dc, ★ work Cluster in next dc, (ch 3, work Cluster in same st) twice, ch 1, skip next dc, sc in next dc, ch 3, skip next dc, sc in next dc, ch 1, skip next dc; repeat from ★ around; join with slip st to top of Beginning Cluster: 150 Clusters and 250 sps.

Rnd 12: Ch 4, [(dc, ch 1) 3 times in next ch-3 sp, dc in next Cluster, ch 1] twice, dc in next ch-1 sp, sc in next ch-3 sp, dc in next ch-1 sp, ch 1, ★ † dc in next Cluster, ch 1, [(dc, ch 1) twice in next ch-3 sp, dc in next Cluster, ch 1] twice, dc in next ch-1 sp, sc in next ch-3 sp, dc in next ch-1 sp, ch 1 †, repeat from † to † across to next corner 3-Cluster group, dc in next Cluster, ch 1, [(dc, ch 1) 3 times in next ch-3 sp, dc in next Cluster, ch 1] twice, dc in next ch-1 sp, sc in next ch-3 sp, dc in next ch-1 sp, ch 1; repeat from ★ 2 times **more**, then repeat from † to † across; join with slip st to first dc: 408 sps.

Rnd 13: Slip st in first ch-1 sp, ch 1, sc in same sp, ch 3, (sc in next ch-1 sp, ch 3) 7 times, decrease, † sc in next ch-1 sp, (ch 3, sc in next ch-1 sp) 5 times, decrease †, repeat from † to † 9 times **more**, ch 3, (sc in next ch-1 sp, ch 3) 8 times, decrease, repeat from † to † 13 times, ch 3, (sc in next ch-1 sp, ch 3) 8 times, decrease, repeat from † to † 10 times, ch 3, (sc in next ch-1 sp, ch 3) 8 times, decrease, repeat from † to † 13 times, ch 3; join with slip st to first sc, finish off.

6. CHARMING

Finished Size: 34" x 46"

MATERIALS
Sport Weight Yarn:
    19 ounces, (540 grams, 1,520 yards)
Crochet hook, size H (5.00 mm) **or** size needed
    for gauge

GAUGE: In pattern, one repeat = 3¼";
          8 rows = 3½"

Gauge Swatch: 6"w x 3"h
Ch 29 **loosely**.
Work same as Afghan Body for 6 rows.
Finish off.

STITCH GUIDE

> **PICOT**
> Ch 3, slip st in top of sc just made.

AFGHAN BODY
Ch 119 **loosely**, place marker in fourth ch from hook
for st placement.

Row 1: Sc in sixth ch from hook, ch 5, skip next 5 chs,
sc in next ch, ★ (ch 3, skip next 2 chs, sc in next ch) 3
times, ch 5, skip next 5 chs, sc in next ch; repeat from
★ across to last 2 chs, ch 2, skip next ch, hdc in last ch:
31 sps.

Row 2 (Right side)**:** Ch 1, turn; sc in first hdc, 9 dc
in next ch-5 sp, ★ sc in next ch-3 sp, (ch 3, sc in next
ch-3 sp) twice, 9 dc in next ch-5 sp; repeat from ★ across
to last sc, skip last sc and next 2 chs, sc in next ch: 95 sts
and 14 ch-3 sps.

Row 3: Ch 6 **(counts as first dc plus ch 3)**, turn;
skip next 3 dc, sc in next dc, ch 3, skip next dc, sc in
next dc, ch 3, ★ sc in next ch-3 sp, ch 5, sc in next
ch-3 sp, ch 3, skip next 4 sts, sc in next dc, ch 3, skip
next dc, sc in next dc, ch 3; repeat from ★ across to last
4 sts, skip next 3 dc, dc in last sc: 31 sps.

Row 4: Ch 4 **(counts as first hdc plus ch 2)**, turn;
sc in first ch-3 sp, (ch 3, sc in next ch-3 sp) twice, ★ 9 dc
in next ch-5 sp, sc in next ch-3 sp, (ch 3, sc in next
ch-3 sp) twice; repeat from ★ across to last dc, ch 2, hdc
in last dc: 89 sts and 18 sps.

Row 5: Ch 5 **(counts as first dc plus ch 2)**, turn;
skip first ch-2 sp, sc in next ch-3 sp, ch 5, sc in next
ch-3 sp, ★ ch 3, skip next 4 sts, sc in next dc, ch 3, skip
next dc, sc in next dc, ch 3, sc in next ch-3 sp, ch 5, sc
in next ch-3 sp; repeat from ★ across to last 2 sts, ch 2,
skip next sc, dc in last hdc: 31 sps.

Row 6: Ch 1, turn; sc in first dc, skip next ch-2 sp,
9 dc in next ch-5 sp, ★ sc in next ch-3 sp, (ch 3, sc in
next ch-3 sp) twice, 9 dc in next ch-5 sp; repeat from ★
across to last 2 sts, skip next sc, sc in last dc: 95 sts and
14 ch-3 sps.

Repeat Rows 3-6 until Afghan Body measures
approximately 37" from beginning ch, ending by working
Row 3; do **not** finish off.

EDGING
Rnd 1: Ch 1, turn; sc in first dc, 4 sc in next ch-3 sp,
3 sc in each sp across to last ch-3 sp, 4 sc in last ch-3 sp,
sc in last dc, place marker around sc just made for st
placement; work 137 sc evenly spaced across end of
rows; working across beginning ch, sc in marked ch,
remove marker and place marker around sc just made
for st placement, 3 sc in next sp, 5 sc in next sp, ★ 2 sc
in next sp, 3 sc in next sp, 2 sc in next sp, 5 sc in next
sp; repeat from ★ across to last sp, 3 sc in last sp, sc in
ch at base of last hdc, place marker around sc just made
for st placement; work 137 sc evenly spaced across end
of rows; join with slip st to Back Loop Only of first sc
(Fig. 1, page 1): 468 sc.

Rnd 2: Ch 1, do **not** turn; working in Back Loops
Only, 2 sc in same st, ★ sc in each sc across to next
marked sc, 3 sc in marked sc, remove marker; repeat
from ★ 2 times **more**, sc in each sc across and in same
st as first sc; join with slip st to Back Loop Only of first
sc: 476 sc.

Rnd 3: Ch 1, working in Back Loops Only, 2 sc in
same st, ★ sc in each sc across to center sc of next
corner 3-sc group, 3 sc in center sc; repeat from ★
2 times **more**, sc in each sc across and in same st as first
sc; join with slip st to Back Loop Only of first sc: 484 sc.

Rnd 4: Ch 1, working in Back Loops Only, 2 sc in
same st, ★ sc in each sc across to center sc of next
corner 3-sc group, 3 sc in center sc; repeat from ★
2 times **more**, sc in each sc across and in same st as first
sc; join with slip st to **both** loops of first sc: 492 sc.

Rnd 5: Ch 5, working in both loops, dc in same st,
ch 2, ★ skip next 2 sc, (dc in next sc, ch 2, skip next
2 sc) across to center sc of next corner 3-sc group, (dc,
ch 2) 3 times in center sc; repeat from ★ 2 times **more**,
skip next 2 sc, (dc in next sc, ch 2, skip next 2 sc) across,
dc in same st as first dc, ch 2; join with slip st to first dc:
172 dc.

Rnd 6: Ch 1, sc in same st, ch 5, ★ (sc in next dc, ch 5)
across to next corner dc, (sc, ch 5) twice in corner dc;
repeat from ★ 2 times **more**, (sc in next dc, ch 5) across,
sc in same st as first sc, ch 2, dc in first sc to form last
ch-5 sp: 176 ch-5 sps.

Rnds 7-11: Ch 1, sc in same sp, work Picot, ch 5,
★ (sc in next ch-5 sp, work Picot, ch 5) across to next
corner ch-5 sp, (sc, work Picot, ch 5) twice in corner
ch-5 sp; repeat from ★ 2 times **more**, (sc in next
ch-5 sp, work Picot, ch 5) across, sc in same sp as first
sc, work Picot, ch 2, dc in first sc to form last ch-5 sp.

Rnd 12: Ch 1, sc in same sp, ch 5, ★ (sc in next
ch-5 sp, ch 5) across to next corner ch-5 sp, (sc, ch 5)
twice in corner ch-5 sp; repeat from ★ 2 times **more**,
(sc in next ch-5 sp, ch 5) across, sc in same sp as first sc,
ch 5; join with slip st to first sc, finish off.

Show us what you're working on!

Share your project photos with us on social media.
Tag us @leisureartsinc or use #leisurearts

1

PLANNER 2025